Clan..

The organic laws realistic courts to fit at and fill to you but details my demon.

There are trickers and lairs.

They fit at some but hide their lies.

Those pretend for relevance all are china soft despotic.

They made a very bad thresholds for HONG KONG common polls for C.E.O by what may be.

What are futures for HONG KONG democracy.

Some reliability are moral asking.

Laws might raw.

Claims that set should something must.

But China clamp you down or clip your words that may addressing.

China tyrants tyranny must a commie clan.

Crow the world so when worlds did fail.

Life can have tangent marks as lies.

CHINABASIC LAWS MAY BE SOME.

China tyrants tyranny jobs have tangent marks but we are still title yes.

They are fierce and forceful.

How as forcible feeble that nay be

Or always china win at wars and battles.

Are there still world justice.

What are fair beside China FELLATRIX.

Do female winningly P.L.A have been blown down.

What make sexes.

What to love should be.

Comb the one who comb the heads of others.

Nemesis cannot be avoid.

Are they china tyrants.

Moral.....
Being so earnest are great and big.

China tyrants egos and wills are
cases that have to obey.

Very despotic is china tyrants ways.

Things to own are china tyranny ways.

Lay our life for sake of foolish worships.

Appeal for peoples all are living.

However evil doers as china leaders
some could kill the innocents.

Sorts of crimes are all with bad fames
and just are China tyrant tyranny.

Gold can stand the tests of fires and

bent and survive with hells.

Only answers boomerang to China
basic tyranny are damned to hell.

To be disturbed are China teams of tyranny
names something not upright.

Then that provoke troubles carry out by
many others for justices.

Marxism says modest to vice is not virtues.

For China tyrants are there are nemesises.

Of courses not all of us are simple minds or
or all thumbs.

Heart may rest but evil doers come so wild
or run amok.

Full of evils are tyrants minds.

Carefree and joys may very much for formative world as UNCLE SAM does.

Can make our minds so right are moral hearts.

But please fewer mental calculations but human right.

Threats from within are so bad.

That are China tyranny to us.

Our guys are fall as scapegoats.

When see my girl can I releas.

When treat by China tyrants or officers or nabobs can I groan or weep.

Who reward those good but punish
evil doers.

Largess gifts are crimes for sale.

Bloody moneys hot and cold are many.

Pull on ways are mandatede henchman.

Henry FOX FAMILY is smuggle groups
but now is china and HONGKONG
congress men.

They are also nabobs that so rich that keep a
place within the ten top most riches in
HONG KONG.

Henry FOX did died some years ago.

FOX JAN TENT is his son.

Sales...

Largess gifts are bribery takes and buys
as sales.

You are cop then you can get the weights in
grams much heavily for each gram you buy.

Ten grams a bag but you get thirty more.

There are so many fellow feels so you
can take.

They call your granny mom the mistress.

You get much more from their head
calculations.

Life worship..

Tyranny natons all have one identity for
each of their people character as those
each people being brain washed.

There are instinct one for logo and hyper-
plug.

Are all are instinct herds.

Are there are blind worship.

Hard to belief that they are right.

Are they sub-human.

Are they sub-able.

Who are able to love many others.

Real to proclaim are justices and
human loves.

But sokmetimes there are few.

Relations connected with lackey kisses
have phenomena.

Principles or mass psychology.

Appearance they have loves but right
relations that they are tyrants may kill
us.

Connected relations all so real but some
are cooked or juggled histories.

Juggled histories are china tyranny stunts.

Lay your claptrap and stupid as fruits
with nuts and evil as evil doers.

Construe our world and seek our hearts
of gold.

Construe our world and know our right and
precious it.

We are human creatures.

We know our worlds.

What for salvation is.

What is nemesis.

What are tyranny.

Turn to life as that always lag also regress.

HONG KONG PEOPLES LIFE REGRESS
TO GOVERN BY BOSSY CHINA SO
TIMES ARE LAG AND POOR.

Logic..........
Logic thoughts are bad to contradicted
but sometimes good to contrariwise
with irony.

Speak in opposite are ways are cynic to
antic and lives have inverted snobbish.

Some are contrastive.

Yes with titles but to see you are so wrong.

Teach you a lesson and stop you to do the
vice are logic and right.

Experiences in total is total are humble
yielding otherwise we may being killed by
China tyrants.

Or we get the fly high careerism or jobs.
No blows of killing cashes hot or cold if no

blow jobs.

VA VA VOOM is sounds of cars.

LAAGERS, LAAGERS China tanks that fire and kill those bare hands and nothing armed china protested pupils such those innocent.

Howl and vow are peoples struggles.

Be a great believer of truth is logic is life.

Registers of lives should sound with logical thoughts.

Compile...
Just compressed and squeezed us
so wrong .

What comprised and being compiled are
forces setting us.

Can we fight for right.

Compromise between good and evil
and right and wrong could bad.

If you are good as saints and do us good
then you are being praise and worship.

However why with you so bad but we have
to compromise with.

It is a bit too thick for china tyranny
and sinful killings.
Who are worth and deserve to be killed.

Compatibility...
There should be no such things for good
common poll compatibility.

China has threshold by controls of common
poll.

They lie and trick by bad threshold.

HONG KONG common polls are fake
and follow bad laws.

China laws that is bad can control the
threshold of common polls.

Common poll in future mostly is fake
and no sexy.

Most candidates that people favor could not
pass the trickery pass one before go to

select by the publics.

There are only mostly leftish political controlled groups can choose the candidates for polling acquiant.

For life set as title yes.

For life if only or but no NAND then how can we stop the wrong.

Some must criticize the evil doers as china tyrants teams.

We have blind faiths obedience..

Docility obedience and fawning are some peoples characters.
After brains washing and tyrants white washing there are expected obedience are then.

Does...

Be a bit weak and spoiled if we stop to criticize our china tyranny.

They pull on rank and do the wrong.

No well developed democrat or true common polls.

Argue so many but tyrant leaders ill in minds.

Just we boo and we are right.

Soft and hard despotic or stick carrots are bad.

Just inquire and after our well being and blesses are rights.

Images that imprint in brains should be fine.

Memory is good for thinking.

Cognitive powers could be done if diligent.

Knowledge about our worlds made our ways.

Fellow feels and social connections just are essays.

Gods are fake and could not transcend any truths of true sciences.

Science might be right for big bang as universal cosmogony.

Triumphant beasts are china tyranny beastly leaders.

How to hide as hypocrites are such and so.

Just beat around the bushes as there are china tricks.

Mild independent subjects are sometimes there should we embrace truths and facts.

Free for speaks or news presses or reports are such.

Much illusions are greedy minds that ma.,

Who belief in substances may well off one day.

What belief in loves may get loves and happliness.

What enlighten primes or keys of lives
are truths.

Thinking is judge-ment and judging can be
acts.

Am I worry much.

There are also always sins and nature sins
are some.

Often sins are cause you wink your eyes but
ignore something that may cause harms and
bad effects to some other in someways and
you do not endeavor to do the good things
for all peoples.
Do not do and keep everything all to be fair
and nothing but fair.
Do not favor those that may such be unfair.
We thus all have often sins.

Sciences...'
China leaders obscurantism come and come
are ways to treat their china peoples.

Sciences are good and often not intuition-
ism but wise and talents brains storms and
many trails and errors also.

There should be lots of testing also.

Lives could be strong if your dare to see and
seek your adventures.

Life can be calm and simple but however
tour de forces are ways of scienes.

Theorems of energies can do a lot.

Sciences are very important.

Medical cares and treats and curse favor all of us.

Sciences can help us to enrich our ways of lives.

They also may give us LONGIVITY.

They could give us pleasures and comforts.

They are sometimes alike to extend our arms and wills and lives.

Cat can look at queen.

But what commie disciples look at.

What to publicize are what to brag.

China high officers pull on ranks.

The summit conference are much commie lairs and   pretenders.

What are hypocrites.

ME-ME-ME syndromes are there.

Ultra leftists as leaders tops are trend to oppress their peoples more.

What to treat the global worlds may keep their own fringe benefits.

Elysian fields know our woelds.

Who give us happiness.

China totalitarian all are evils.

All the eyes could see as navel gazing must be so wrong.

What can they see.

Come and treat me no tyranny and set us free.
However men could be navigable when tamed and brains washed.
Future ordinance 23 are something catchy to us.
It may lead us follow those absolute powers. Commie toying us with bad laws so mad.

Ways..
Widen ways are moral notions.

Wits and wills are minds to process some of
our common senses.

Claim our ways so good and also may laws
abide.

Human understanding just have axioms of
ways.

Species of beauty something buy.

Buy our ways that good but might not sell.

Simple lives still need definitions just by
good judgments.

But how to examine our histories so fair
with fair plays should be fair games.

Logic deduct ways are not the only ways that we could sensed or felt.

Few sybaritic but do the rights

Logical thoughts will also need synthetic beside analytic.